The Price Is Right

Blair Ballin

The Price Is Right.

Printed by:
90-Minute Books
302 Martinique Drive
Winter Haven, FL 33884
www.90minutebooks.com

Published in the United States of America

Book ID: 140604-001

ISBN-13: 978-0692651759
ISBN-10: 0692651756

Here's What's Inside…

Scottsdale, Arizona
August 2015

Note from the Author:

When I first started in real estate sales, I made it part of my mission to learn from some of the most successful real estate people in the business so I could provide the highest value to my clients. Several years ago, I was part of a real estate coaching program where I heard the following phrase, "Price is only a factor in the absence of value." This phrase has stuck with me ever since, and allows me to set myself apart from many of my colleagues.

In my opinion, there are 2 types of agents: one that thinks a home not selling is only related to price; and the other agent who understands marketing, market forces, data and statistics, and realizes price is only one of many factors in accomplishing a home sale.

The agent that thinks price is the only issue really bothers me. They do a disservice to the industry. Unfortunately, we have an industry-wide issue where many homeowners are misinformed and undereducated. If we are doing our jobs as fiduciaries for our clients, I think we have to look beyond the price to help the homeowners get the most value for their homes. This comes from 2 places: laziness or ignorance. Many times it takes more than just a post in the yard to sell a home. More work is required. The lazy agents sit back, and wait for an offer. When it doesn't arrive, they resort to the price-drop method. The other is ignorance. If all they know is if a home doesn't sell, all they will do is drop the price. They might not be aware of the things that are needed to help sell a home—other than price.

Maybe it is a price problem, or maybe that agent isn't creating enough value for the home. Maybe they should be asking themselves not how they can get their clients to drop their asking prices, but rather what they need to do to create the value so buyers will want to pay the asking prices.

It's been my passion ever since that fateful day to do what I can to help my clients get as much money as possible for their houses, and to educate homeowners about their options. I was recently interviewed for a segment during which I discussed how to educate homeowners on how to sell their homes for the most money possible and how to avoid hiring price-driven agents whose main agendas were selling houses quickly or to just reduce the price when facing adversity.

For the Realtors reading this book, please know that my greatest wish is to raise the bar. I see this as a game changer. You will hear me talk about being outstanding. Excellence no longer is the bar. Outstanding is.

This is a book written by a Realtor discussing marketing tactics, and to help educate. The philosophies are applicable for almost all businesses. Create the value and people will pay for it.

My legacy is greater than selling a home or helping someone accomplish their goals. I want to make a positive change in our industry. I want to leave a positive impression for those that I work with now, will work with, and those that come after us. Let us remember who comes first-the client.

Learn the 6 words to empower you, and enjoy the Book!

To Your Success!

Blair Ballin

Price Isn't The Problem. You Are.

Susan: Good afternoon. This is Susan Austin. I'm excited to be here with Blair Ballin. Blair is going to be sharing with us his thoughts and ideas on how to empower homeowners against price-driven real estate agents. Welcome, Blair!

Blair: Thank you so much, Susan. I'm very excited and glad to be here.

Susan: Why did you want to write a book on empowering homeowners against price-driven agents?

Blair: I was part of a Facebook real estate group and the question, "What do I need to do to market my listing so it will sell?" was asked.

Most of the Realtors' answers were to drop the price. I became very agitated and wanted to voice my opinion so homeowners would know this, and that they could do something about it. That laid the foundation for this book.

I'm not suggesting a home's list price isn't important when selling a home. It certainly is. I am saying that there are other factors that come into the equation too, and many times some Realtors don't know how to handle those, or have no clue what they are. The homeowner should be educated and empowered to know that they don't have to automatically accept a price reduction. Price should not always be the focus. But let's eliminate other checkboxes, and then if need be, reduce the price.

Susan: Homeowners aren't educated enough about what to look for in agents when they go to sell their homes?

Blair: That's correct, and I believe a lot of that is because of the real estate community. It's time we be outstanding. Excellence is no longer the top of the line. We are in a period of time where we have so many tools at our disposal to use. It's time we step up. Some agents place the sign in the yard, take pictures and have a video done. That's a start but there's a lot more to it than that. What are your obligations when you sell? What is required of you? These are some of the things you need to be educated about upfront. When I sold my first home, I basically thought I list it, get an offer, do some repairs and close. There's much more to it than that, and we need to make the public and our clients aware of those things. In the fast paced society we now live in, everyone involved in the transaction can get caught up in the emotions of whatever event occurs. While that can happen, it is important to not forget which side you represent as an agent, and making sure that the client is receiving the representation they deserve. Dotting those i's and crossing those t's is imperative. Carefully going over all documents is crucial. We have come to use e-sign programs, and a lot of times, signing things just happens without explanations. Please do not ever sign something you are not sure about. I believe most issues come about from lack of effective communication. Texting, emailing, and Facebooking all remove proper ways of communication.

Agent Tip:

To ensure a greater success rate for making sure a deal closes – Pick up the phone, and talk. You would be amazed at how many issues come about from the other agent making an assumption from your tone in your email. Own it. Talk about it. Get it resolved. The end result usually will be so incredibly worth it.

(Note from Author)-Throughout the book, I will be providing: problems, case studies, and power tips. Please pay special attention to these important points.

Problem #1- Many agents don't know how to correctly compare properties to establish an accurate list price.

Case Study #1- 2014. I met an expired listing homeowner – a listing that didn't sell. And yes, most agents will tell you it didn't sell because it was overpriced. Please don't accept that as fact. My client had a home directly across the street from a home with the same floorplan, almost same everything – except that one did not have mountain views. It was listed at $355,000 and under contract.

The homeowners were very motivated to sell, but they were unhappy with the price others were quoting them. I did my research and felt a list price of $415,000 was supported. A list price of $60,000, more than the same model match home across the street? I believe the neighbor's Realtor did not know how to create value. I do not quote "high" prices to obtain business. I just feel that many times I can find the value, and justify it. The value was far greater than the mountain views. It was understanding market conditions and area statistics, combined with the home's features that allowed me to be confident in the pricing we established. We sold the home for $390,000. Still $35,000 more than the neighbor's home. And I felt like I educated the clients correctly, and when presented properly, the market accepted.

Problem # 2- The Post & Pray Method. Have you heard of it before? The Realtor puts a sign post in your yard, puts the listing in MLS and then prays your home will sell. Don't get me wrong, I put up a sign, and I pray, but I am an outstanding agent and do a lot more too.

What can be done:

Blair's Power Tips:

• Facebook-targeted ad, which, while it may be done with a few clicks, it isn't done by most Realtors. Facebook now lets you run an ad to consumers based on their net worth, where they live, and what they do. WOW!

(Note from the Author)-As Facebook continues to advance, these strategies continue to improve their effectiveness.

• Drone video. An expansive view of a lush backyard with a serene sunset is captivating. Pictures don't do justice like a video does. Many Midwesterners tired of the cold salivate over our clear skies, and picturesque sunsets. A video can be powerful.

• Professional pictures. How many IPhone pictures have you seen marketing a home online? My reaction is to laugh. If that's your home, do you want the viewer to laugh? Almost anyone can have professional pictures taken-even a For Sale By Owner. But, is your picture being marketed correctly? Does it have the most effective SEO with it? A pretty picture with the right SEO is worth a thousand searches ☺

4

• It sounds simple, but, correct research on pricing. Not everyone knows how. Some people still use the price per square foot method. HA! This is a very dated model of comparison and very rarely is it accurate. Example-You have 3 home sales, and your home as the "subject" property. If one sold for $100/sq ft, one for $50/sq ft, and one for $75/sq ft- that makes your home worth $75/sq ft based on that model. By doing that you could have just lost out on $25/sq ft. Please do not use the price per square foot model.

• The comparative approach is usually far more accurate. What did those 3 homes have that you do not-subtract that from their sale price. What do you have that those homes do not have-add that in to their sale price. Keep in mind if the top sale in an area is $100,000, it is harder to sell your home (no matter how more upgraded) for a lot more – especially if there is an appraisal involved. Yes, prices have to go up at some point, but just because you have a $10,000 pool doesn't mean your home is now worth $110,000...always. Your Realtor should know market trends for pools in that price range in that area to offer an opinion of value that is supported to allow your home to sell for the correct amount.

Why Marketing Is the Key to Putting More Money in Your Pocket

Susan: Are you suggesting that better marketing can make a house more valuable?

Blair: Absolutely, 100% yes. If I expose your home to more qualified buyers and prospects, then I'm going to create a better value for your home. Price is a function of supply and demand. Effective marketing increases demand.

Example: Barrett-Jackson, the world-famous car auction house. Their auction has created an atmosphere that results in more car buyers bidding against each other to buy the cars they are interested in. Whether it involves ego, or just getting caught up in the bidding process, the buyer wants the car because there is a perceived value. It is a brilliant marketing practice.

When it comes to houses, your Realtor must know how to create that value for your home. Your home is the product. Once the product is marketed correctly, price becomes less important than value.

Susan: You're suggesting that by homeowners not understanding this, they're leaving cash on the table?

Blair: Absolutely. I feel one of our jobs as Realtors is to educate homeowners. If they pick the right agent to sell their home, then they potentially will put more money in their pockets. Will the home sell just as quickly? It might. If we go back to Case Study 1 -those clients netted $35,000 more in their pocket. I think they were fairly happy with that outcome. And I was confident I did the best job I could have at the time. And just as important, I feel I did the community a good service by making sure pricing was positively affected.

Susan: How did you learn to do your comparables, Blair?

Blair: Back in 2007, I became quickly familiar with what's called a Broker Price Opinion (BPO). It is a bank's way of asking someone to create a value/price for a property. During that 2007-2010 era, I sold a lot of foreclosures. Part of becoming a foreclosure agent involves learning how to comp a property/determine the value. I feel that I treated the bank BPO as if it were a traditional or regular homeowner asking me to create a price/value for them. It didn't matter that the property was "in distress."

I studied appraisals, market conditions, pricing, how homes sold (cash vs financing), days on market, incentives-everything. It was a difficult time because lenders were tighter on lending, and buyers were unsure of the market. My listings sold for top dollar, usually more than others and I very rarely had BPOs returned to me for insufficient data or errors.

The 3 Factors for Establishing the Value of Your Home

Susan: How is price established in the marketplace?

Blair: A couple of different things:

1. Comparables. The other homes for sale and those which have sold recently near your home. Those homes play a very important factor in price.

2. Features and amenities. What do you have and don't have compared to the comparables?

3. Motivation. Do you need to sell right away? If yes, pricing it more aggressively is probably in line. If you have time on your side, you don't want to take yourself out of the market, but maybe you can afford to start "higher."

Then, have a meeting with your agent to discuss all of these factors, and figure out what the best price is for you.

You can also have an appraisal done on your home. I don't normally suggest having one completed though. Some reasons why would be that: certain lenders might not accept it; and it might eliminate certain buyers.

Also, these factors all work together...or they should work together. The right comparables, with the right features, and the having motivation to sell will almost always lead to a sale.

Why Time of Year Doesn't Matter When Selling Your Home

Case Study #2- Surprise, AZ FSBO.

Several years ago I met with a For Sale By Owner (FSBO), someone who is trying to sell their home on their own. This was a very lovely couple that was very motivated to sell, but they didn't have to sell.

I found their advertisement on the internet, and made an appointment to look at the home that afternoon. Their home was in Surprise and for sale for $100,000. I did my market research, and I believed their home was worth $115,000.

During our meeting (which was about 2 weeks before Thanksgiving) I suggested to them to list their home for $115,000. They were shocked because no one else had mentioned this price for them.

This again goes back to finding their right comparables. This was a cookie cutter type community in Surprise, where most of the homes look the same. There were no major differences and I still felt that their home was worth $115,000. They also understood that I could bring the value to the table. They saw that I was an outstanding agent, that I knew the market conditions, and that I knew the market. I understood their situation and was able to put all the pieces together. It was a perfect match. They were great Sellers too. They were willing to listen to my advice, suggestions, and guidance. I don't ask that my sellers always do as I ask – I just ask them to listen. They listened, and the result was incredible.

The couple asked me, "When should we put the home on the market?" They were being told by some Realtors to wait until May. Now, I was shocked. I get it – maybe May and June might be a good time to sell, but I would argue that the January/February time frame is better. In the Phoenix area, there are a lot of motivated buyers during the early part of the year, and there is more demand. In the summer, fewer homes come up for sale, which is good, but there are fewer buyers too. So why wait? My answer to them was that we should list right now. Of course, they responded with, "You mean right after Thanksgiving, right?"

And I said, "No. I mean literally right now, like this evening, right now." They signed the paperwork that evening, and right around the New Year, they got their check from closing. We sold for $110,000.

They netted about $4,000 more with me than they could have if they got their FSBO asking price.

It was all about the marketing. What I haven't told you yet is our home was a model match to the highest sale but we backed a main road and weren't as upgraded. My systematic approach still allowed my client's home to sell for more than they were even thinking, let alone others. They still wonder what the magic was that I used that allowed me to sell their home for more in a time when most Realtors would say, "Don't put the home on the market because it's Thanksgiving time, and no one is looking." Or, "your home backs a main road; it is 'worth' less." Their review of my service is on Zillow. I encourage you to check it out.

It's not magic. It's marketing. If your agent doesn't know how to market your home correctly, then, yes, the time of year will matter. If they do know how to market it correctly, the time of year won't matter, for the most part. There are days and times that aren't good to put a home on the market, but for the most part, there are Realtors who believe that certain months, seasons, and days are not good, and I would strongly disagree. I believe this FSBO example is an example, and not the exception. In the Greater Phoenix area in the winter months, yes, fewer homes sell but there are still plenty that do. Ask your Realtor for stats that show how many homes are listed compared to selling to other months. My opinion is you will be shocked, and realize you might not want to miss out on that valuable marketing time.

Why Some Homes Just Don't Sell

Susan: Why do you think that some homes just don't sell?

Blair: It's going to depend on so many different factors. A few of those are:

1. The market
2. Market conditions
3. Price
4. The Realtor
5. The marketing

And then there are just some instances where it might be a very specific product that will take longer to sell.

For example, $10,000,000 Phoenix homes sell quite less frequently than $10,000,000 homes do in Southern California.

Blair's Power Tips:

1-Staging

Staging is key. Is your home staged correctly? Staging a home does play a role in selling, pricing, and the whole package. And staging doesn't have to cost you an arm and a leg. There are very affordable options to not break your bank account.

What if your home isn't selling but it isn't staged right? Should you do a price reduction? Maybe. But why not stage it correctly first, and then, if it hasn't sold, determine if better staging would make the difference. I think you would be surprised at the result.

2- Energy

I'm a believer in energy. Maybe there's just bad energy in the home. Maybe you don't want to sell and buyers are picking up on that. I am fairly confident if that is the case that selling your home will be harder. Have you heard about planting a St. Joseph statue upside down in your backyard? Some people do it, and their home sells. I am sure some people do it and their home doesn't sell too, but the point is energy stuff can work. If anything, at least it will make you be more confident in your home sale. Just being more positive will help things. Believe me, that happens quite often – a home is correctly priced, the agent is doing everything in their power to get the home sold, it's marketed correctly, it's priced correctly, but there's just bad energy around the home. That home will not sell. Price can be irrelevant in that scenario.

Why Your Realtor Could Be the Problem

Susan: The agents who are hounding the homeowners to always be lowering their price, why do you think they're doing that so often?

Blair: I think it's a combination of possibly not knowing what else to do, not wanting to do it, not wanting to pay for it, or being lazy. This book is meant to empower homeowners against the price-driven Realtor, but it's also meant to educate Realtors that it's time we be outstanding. Keep learning your trade. Keep learning what other businesses are doing to succeed and help sell their products. It's not just about dropping the price.

I want to touch on something quickly: "neighborhood experts." Some neighborhood experts, in my opinion, get a name for themselves by selling lots of homes quickly. If price is not sacrificed, this is great. It's when homes are being undervalued/priced and sold fast causing a negative trend in the area that I have an issue with and question. I really believe they are costing the homeowners thousands of dollars because I feel they are underpricing their list prices and they do not educate their homeowners, and then the homes sell fast. Anyone can sell an iPhone for $50; not everyone can sell it for $600.

In the end, all the homeowners have really done is hire someone who has sold a home for, or listed a home for less, and not done much in the marketing space.

I don't know that they really are experts. I'm not saying that no community or neighborhood expert out there isn't one, but I think most homeowners are doing themselves an injustice by just saying, "Let's call the neighborhood specialist because they sold another home around the corner." Unfortunately, I think that's happening more than we'd care to admit in the industry. It needs to change.

Blair's Power Tips:

1. Interview multiple agents if you feel something isn't right. It is my belief interviewing more than 3 is not necessary. If you feel good about 1, that is all you need.

2. Review all neighborhood statistics. This is a must. You've heard me say numerous times how important the right comparables are. Statistics go hand in hand with that. Make sure you have all the data.

Susan: Is this a self-perpetuating problem? Homeowner A sells their house for less, and then it's a lower comp for the next house, and so on?

Blair: Yes, but remember my sale for $390,000? Great systems and marketing can reverse that problem. Now their neighbor will try to sell for more, and the next and the next. But there is a possibility had the "expert" in the area listed the home it might not have sold for that and caused the opposite effect.

Price Is Only a Factor in the Absence of Value

Susan: You speak, Blair, about the marketing piece that you offer that a lot of agents don't. Can you share with the homeowner who doesn't quite understand some of the jargon you use- what it is you are doing in terms of marketing beyond putting the sign in the front yard, putting the home in the MLS, putting together a pretty flyer, and sending a postcard out to the neighborhood to advertise? What is the homeowner not seeing that you're doing and that the typical agent isn't doing?

Blair: Great question. Let me tie this back to the whole premise of the book, which is, "Price is only a factor in the absence of value." To create that value, you have to study the market, and that itself is a marketing tool that should be able to get the Realtor and the homeowner more for the home. If we take that away, what else is there for actual marketing?

1. Internet. This is a whole book in itself. It depends on the house and location. Getting top search engine placement. Being featured on major search sites like Zillow, Realtor.com, etc.

2. Facebook. Facebook is a very heavily used and consumer-driven tool right now. The problem is it is not used correctly. Just putting a status out there that says, "Hey, it's Blair. I have a new listing for sale in Chandler or Scottsdale" isn't really going to do a client any good.

3. Flyers. Let me touch on flyers for a moment. A pretty flyer in a mailbox really does you no good. Unless there is some way to track it, all you are doing is giving information out. There's nothing wrong with giving information, but you are trying to sell your home. You want to know what is and isn't working. Without a tracking mechanism, flyers in a tube are useless.

4. Open Houses. Most agents put up 5 signs, and sit at your coffee table watching a football game. We put out (usually) over 50 signs, have 2 big flags, multiple video advertisements, online advertising, sometimes letting the neighbors know through door knocking efforts, and we now use a "skydancer" to create a big neighborhood event. This has a 10x effect on traffic.

As you know by now, I create value by marketing. When we list a homeowner's home for sale, the product is the house, not me. If I want to create more qualified prospects, just putting a status on Facebook saying "Hey, look at this home I just listed," I might get a couple of likes and comments but I am not promoting the home – I am promoting me. Instead, I create a campaign marketing the home. Even if it is just a status update, why not check into the home and get some SEO benefit by putting the address, or asking "Who do you know that is looking to live in Gilbert?"

Furthermore, here in my area, we get quite a few people who move here, and/or purchase here from different areas like the Midwest, or even a little bit further north in Canada. So, ads in those areas are very beneficial.

Blair's Power Tips:

Create those online campaigns to attract those consumers. If you're on Facebook, then consider running ads in those areas – to Realtors and the public. Facebook is a marketer's dream. The cost and ability to market to specifically who you want/need is a dream come true. And sometimes it can even be free!

If we think that the consumer's going to be coming from a trade show or a horse show (we have the world-famous Arabian Horse Show here in Scottsdale), go to the Arabian Horse Show and have a booth to make sure that that listing is featured there. Whatever the right tools are, the agent needs to understand the market and be aggressive in pursuit.

Susan: There's a lot of thought that goes into the marketing. I take it that not every home is marketed the same way.

Blair: Absolutely. When I meet with homeowners, I have my "standard" presentation, but then from there everything is custom tailored to them, and the home. It would be highly ineffective to have a standard plan for everyone. We have systematic procedures in place for efficiency as a baseline but custom tactics are added to each home.

Note From Author:

Marketing is one of my passions. Having someone believe in me to help sell their home is something I take very seriously. When I list a home for sale I try all methods I can think of to increase qualified demand to that home. When I do that, the sale is imminent.

How to Pick the Right Agent to Sell Your Home

Susan: The homeowner who wants to meet with a Realtor to find out if they're a good fit for selling their home, what do they need to know?

Blair: There's some preliminary research that they can do online, such as going to Zillow to find out about agents. Zillow also provides a "Zestimate," an online value of a home. I would use this information as data in making your decision, but do not accept it as the actual number for your home. And more importantly, price/value should not be the reason you hire anyone. Hire someone because they bring value to you.

The Questions You Should Ask: The Historic Questions and why some of them don't mean much

1. What's your average days on the market? I guess this could matter if every agent truly had the most accurate number for this. What if an agent relisted a home to make the days show as less? What if the home wasn't listed in MLS until an offer was accepted? These types of stats/numbers don't always portray what really happened. They should not be used in deciding on an agent.

2. What's your list to sale price? HA! For an agent that underlists everything and then the property sells for more, sure it sold for more, but it was underpriced. Or, what if a home's price was raised to offset closing costs? Does that mean the agent did a

better job? Maybe, but does that make them the right choice for you?

3. How many homes have you sold in the area? Personally, I am not sure why this matters. What if I live in the area, know it inside and out, but choose to not work in it? The systems, tools, and market knowledge an agent has are key. Just because an agent sold a certain number of homes in an area doesn't make them the expert. What if 1 investor listed 10 homes with an agent in 1 area, and that agent never stepped foot in any of them, and knew nothing about them?

4. What will you do for marketing? How much will you spend marketing my home? YES!

5. How did you arrive at the price you are quoting me? YES!

6. If the home doesn't sell at our price, what will happen next? YES!

7. Where will you market my home to? YES!

I am extremely passionate about this. I also believe there are so many myths and old-school type questions and methods that don't cut it anymore. I get a kick out of the agent boasting about selling a home for 109% of list price. I read that as they underpriced it. Not always, but why would it sell for more? Sure, sometimes buyers pay more for a home. And yes, you can create an auction and some buyers would pay more, and you have done your job. However, I am willing to bet that on most occasions that did not happen.

When you meet with your Realtor, ask them to show you the search that they did to find/use the comparables. This will show you exactly what they are using. Maybe they missed a certain part of your area. Maybe they didn't know which areas to search. If they know the market, and area they should know exactly where to search.

Sometimes agents do searches by subdivision names. By doing so, you are relying on others spelling correctly. A map based search will likely always be more accurate – it eliminates possible spelling errors. If a homeowner's subdivision is Grayhawk, and a Realtor spells it "Greyhawk," and your agent has searched by Grayhawk you could be missing out on a comparable that would make a huge difference. The continued problem is that some agents don't own that mistake. And I don't mean the one who spelled it incorrectly. The agent who did the search for you should have done the correct search. Be outstanding. Dig deep. Check and confirm everything. It's not only your job but the only acceptable standard.

The Role Condition Plays in Creating Value

Susan: How much does the condition of the home play into the price? Do you think some homeowners think their house is a bit more fabulous than it is?

Blair: Condition absolutely plays a role, but when it comes to saying what percentage it plays, that's a very tough question to answer. I feel that many agents could say, "Price would be a factor of condition, or condition a factor of price," and then you could price it accordingly. If there are a lot of investors looking to buy and the condition of the home isn't that great, but it could be fixed up and flipped that has its own value to the right buyer.

I don't think agents should use condition as the most important factor to say, "Well, your house is a dump. It needs to be priced lower." This plays a role in the decision, but it's not the most important factor.

Susan: Do you coach the homeowners on the things they could do to make their home more desirable?

Blair: I do. That's part of the service that I offer. Using the $110,000 Surprise home from before -- it was in a perfectly livable condition, but it wasn't upgraded like some of the other homes in the area. There were a couple of things I saw that could be done at a very small expense.

The home had a security door and one of the knobs was old and worn. I suggested to the owners to replace that because it would help improve our first impression. Just like replacing or installing new knobs on cabinets – it can make the cabinets look much different and/or new/er.

Susan: That was just pennies to fix.

Blair: Exactly. The idea that we need to spend thousands of dollars to get a home ready for sale is a myth. It might be the case sometimes, but not usually. My focus is on finding ways to spend as little as possible and having the highest return possible. And all improvements should provide ROI in order to be recommended and undertaken.

How to Get Exposure for Your Home Prior to Listing It for Sale

Susan: Let's say I'm a homeowner, and I'm interested in selling in a couple of months – walk me through what your process is for working with someone who wants to sell their home?

Blair: Sure. There are obviously going to be different scenarios. Some people meet with me now but want to sell their homes in a year, or they want to sell next week. The homeowner should do their due diligence to make sure that they've met with the appropriate number of agents. As I mentioned, that can be up to 3. They should call, email, text, and visit websites to find information about Realtors. We offer a pre-marketing program where we can market a home prior to it being placed in MLS. The "coming soon" listings in and of themselves create value to certain buyers -- they get something others can't have.

Susan: I want to thank you because this is very refreshing. I do think that "lower the price" is the knee-jerk reaction agents have when a home doesn't sell. You're saying it's a disservice to just assume that the price is the problem. It may be a price problem, as you pointed out, but you can't assume that it is just because someone's house hasn't sold or they didn't get what they were asking for.

Blair: Often, for example, a home will be listed for two weeks. The Realtor has either been trained, taught, or coached, or they have learned or read, that if after that time it has not gone under contract -the price is high. Then they need to get a price reduction. Now, the homeowner is being reached out to by their agent, who may or may not have done any marketing and told to drop the price. I don't feel that should be the reaction. Maybe the price reduction is needed but has everything else been done that can be done?

This is why I'm so passionate about it and wanted to write this book. Knowing that owners are not informed correctly and are losing out on cash really upsets me. I know that it could have been listed correctly upfront, and probably gotten more money and probably sold by that time, or at least sold for more upfront. I want this to change. I want our industry to be outstanding. And I believe these changes will help.

Susan: Thank you for this, Blair. I really think this is a book that homeowners need to see and read before they list their homes because they're not hearing it elsewhere. Thank you.

Blair: It is and I appreciate the time. Some homeowners who want to sell their homes and look to buy another home right after that may miss out on a bunch of cash from their home sale and not be able to get their next dream home as a result. That's a disservice to them. I do hope that the book empowers those homeowners. I'm very, very passionate about this, and I'm very passionate about my marketing. I tell homeowners when I meet with them that I'm an aggressive marketer who happens to have a real estate license. I feel I bring value to the table.

Going back full circle - if price is only a factor in the absence of value, how do I create that value so the homeowner can get the price they want and need? Call me. I will show you how. It doesn't cost you more. In fact, it will cost you more if you don't.

By reading this book you have empowered yourself to accept more. Don't settle for the "we need to drop the price." You now have the right and power to say the following 6 words, "Price isn't the problem. You are."

Here's How to Get the True Value for Your Home When You Go to Sell

You've checked Zillow, and it says your home is worth less than you think. You've seen a neighbor sell their home recently, but they didn't get as much for it as you thought they should. You want to sell your home, but you don't want to give it away. The confusing part is knowing how to find an agent who isn't going to insist on price reductions at every turn.

That's where I come in. We help people just like you sell your home for its true value, no matter the circumstances.

Step 1: We meet with you to preview your home and offer any staging, de-cluttering, and suggested repairs that we have found that help sell homes more quickly and maximize value.

Step 2: We pull all the comparables for your home, and stats like absorption rate, and share them with you to help pinpoint the value of your home in today's market. You will know exactly how we came up with the price and can have input in the process.

Step 3: We put our systems in place, using our unique marketing to expose your home to the best possible buyers, all the while protecting your interests throughout the entire process.

Now you can sell your home with the systems and strategies for finding the right buyer to pay the true value within the timeframe that works for you.

To schedule a FREE, No Obligation appointment where I can discuss your situation, please call me at 480-233-6433, or visit me on the web at www.BlairBallin.com.